GEMINI

HOROSCOPE

& ASTROLOGY

2020

Gemini

Horoscope & Astrology

2020

Published by Mystic Shores publications

Suite SM-2380-6403

14601 North Bybee Lake Court

Portland, Oregon 97203

Phone: +1 (805) 308-6503

islandauthor@hotmail.com

Acknowledgment:

Thank you to the stargazers, dreamers, and mystics.

You make this world a better place.

2020 is an incredible year of an increased potential for Gemini. The winds of change blow favorably, encouraging new ideas and concepts which inspire growth. Not one, not two, not three, but four Supermoons in 2020 ensures plenty of cosmic energy arrives to inspire Gemini to develop innovative dreams in tune with their wildest ideas and aspirations. There is astonishing progress to be made towards obtaining substantial growth, Gemini utilizes the power of air to steam ahead and make progress on their most lofty goals.

Mercury Retrograde is the most significant destabilizing force in 2020. Forewarned is forearmed and Gemini harnesses the power of their mind to find solutions and take corrective action before relationships veer off course.

2020 is a year which blends the elemental forces of Earth, Air, Fire, and Water with new world technology. This dramatically expands your star signs creative abilities. The Gemini star sign is one of air dominance, and when harnessed correctly, you make remarkable progress towards innovative and idealistic ventures in this most incredible year of potentiality.

With so many compelling reasons to shine, the star sign Gemini can look forward to incredible cosmic energy which helps increase and boost the potential possible in 2020, and beyond.

Gemini

Gemini Dates: May 21 to June 20
Symbol: Twins
Element: Air
Planet: Mercury
House: Third
Colors: Yellow, blue
Lucky Numbers: 2, 16, 18, 21

JANUARY ASTROLOGY

January 3 – First Quarter Moon in Aries.

This Moon phase occurs at 04.45 UTC.

January 3, 4 - Quadrantids Meteor Shower.

The Quadrantids meteor shower run yearly from January 1-5. The Quadrantids meteor shower peaks this year on the night of the 3rd and morning of the 4th.

January 10 - Full Moon in Cancer.

This full moon phase occurs at 19:21 UTC. This full moon is called the Full Wolf Moon because this was the time of year when hungry wolf packs howled outside camps. This full moon has also been known as the Old Moon and the Moon After Yule.

January 10 - Penumbral Lunar Eclipse.

A penumbral lunar eclipse occurs as the Moon passes through the Earth's partial shadow or penumbra. During this type of eclipse, the Moon will darken slightly but won't wholly eclipse. This penumbral eclipse is visible throughout most of Europe, Africa, Asia, and Western Australia.

January 17 – Last Quarter Moon in Libra.

This Moon phase occurs at 12.58 UTC.

January 24 – New Moon in Capricorn.

This new moon phase occurs at 21:42 UTC. The Moon is on the same side of the Earth as the Sun and will not be visible in the night sky. This phase occurs at 21:03 UTC. This is an excellent time to view galaxies and stars as there is no moonlight to obscure your view of the universe.

JANUARY HOROSCOPE

JANUARY WEEK ONE

A happy vibe puts you in the mood to celebrate, you are making strides towards widening your social circle, and this revolutionizes your overall approach to participating in the social events, as you are more willing to put yourself out there and meet new people, find your tribe and embrace diversify your social ties. Your learning that joining forces with others does bring added benefits into your life. It gives you opportunities to blend your energy emotionally with kindred spirits who in turn usher in a new chapter of well-being into your life. You have pushed into bold new frontiers and can level up social opportunities which entice you to expand your horizons. This is a continuation of a broader theme which has been occurring in your life recently. As you push your boundaries back, you are liberated and able to enjoy the extraordinary freedom. You have a long being a slave to structure and definition, this is a chapter which is about dissolving boundaries and having faith that you are being guided forward towards the attainment of happiness with like-minded people.

Additionally, you blaze towards a project which sparks your passion, this venture arrives to kickstart a new phase of potential. It is an essential time for setting bold intentions and planning for ideal outcomes. Setting intentions plants the seeds which will help you turn your dreams into reality. Structuring plans and asserting your needs, creates a beneficial impact, you gain the essence of manifestation through setting clear intentions.

JANUARY WEEK TWO

Your mind is curious and hungry, opening your thoughts to new ideas and information provides you with valuable resources which sharpen your intellect and has you exploring a variety of opportunities. Your mind runs ablaze with fresh inspiration. An adventurous element is inviting you to try new areas and explore options which encourage you to learn a new area. Growing your talents begins a chapter which is prosperous and dazzling. Optimism is a theme which sweeps in to promote growth and expansion. It is an excellent time to launch a venture which has a far-reaching impact on your situation. You are ready to transform and head towards a life which is secure and abundant. Harnessing the power of your mind has a profound effect on your spirit, it is a vitality boosting phase, which motivates you to take on challenges and set ambitious goals. It is a chapter which is richly imbued with self-expression and creativity. As you refine your skills, you chase your dreams and encourage your talents to grow exponentially. This reveals a style which is expressive, unique, and flamboyant. As you progress, you find that sharing your passions with a broader audience provides you with valuable feedback and new leads to explore. This is a necessary time to gather your thoughts and think about where you are headed. Exploring ways to improve your circumstances sees you inspired by innovative areas. The winds of change are ready to tempt you forward. Looking at your life's deeper purpose, you step into an area which provides you with broader options. Life is begging to be explored, you can appreciate the opportunities which flow into your awareness to tantalize your inspiration.

JANUARY WEEK THREE

It's a great time to implement your ideas and get them out there in the broader arena. With luck and fortune sweeping into your life, you can embark on developing your visionary plans or even take steps towards a game-changing venture. Creating a splash among your social vibe helps provide kindred spirits to encourage your growth. Connecting with a like-minded tribe merges your ideas with a flow of inspiration, which is inspired. Creating your unique brand puts a stamp on your vision, which is in alignment with your mindset. You can attract the right kind of attention, your confidence is growing, you can move towards obtaining goals rather than spending your days in an endless rotating circle. Forward motion backs your growth, you can relish the wild and rebellious desires which motivate your energy forward. Excitement and adventure are fuelling a more significant shift in your world. This takes you towards a vital breakthrough and enables you to open a gateway of abundance. Essential changes are set to occur, your focus and determination are instrumental in turning a situation to your advantage. You may have been dealing with a chaotic environment which has left you to have to pick up the threads and completely reorganize your goals. These changes are encouraging you to head towards a situation which draws happiness into your world. Removing the limiting beliefs allows you to let go of the drama, you release old emotions which can scatter to the wind. This is liberating, it does help you gain traction on a vision which is forward facing. You may be feeling torn about heading in a new direction, once you begin this vital transition, you will draw opportunities which support your growth. Staying true to your inner wisdom clears space for a phase which offers many rewards.

JANUARY WEEK FOUR

You build a bridge towards a brighter future, cultivating the attainment of goals allows you to express your natural flair for the original. Brilliant creative ideas and impulses simmer within your spirit, gifted with insightful thoughts, you characterize cutting edge innovation during the phase ahead. You exhibit a strong ability to thrive as your perspective broadens. The vast possibilities which inspire your mind to enable you to tap into a long forgotten dream. Discovering an area of service, your vision and draws sunshine into your world. Taking in a broader picture of what is possible in your situation, you pull harmonizing energy, your ideas are blended with old world charm and new technology. Reawakening to this trailblazing time you combine a combination of logic and emotional awareness, it's the perfect time to merge with your inspiration. Your dedication to achieving a high result is instrumental in setting the right wheel in motion to make your dreams. You're ready to make some changes, putting yourself out in the community leads to an encounter which sparks your interest. It sets the stage for a bountiful time as you enjoy the sharing of ideas and thoughts with another. The more you open yourself to new experiences, the more you see signs of opportunities which arrive to support this phase of personal growth. Building a rapport with another leads to sharing lively discussions and provide you with opportunities to further expand your social horizons. You have an incredible desire for self-expression, and fulfillment, connecting with kindred spirits helps provide you with emotional sustenance during this adventurous time. There is value in getting together with others during this time as it draws harmony and well-being into your surroundings, leading to flow on beneficial effects on your spirit.

February 2 – First Quarter Moon in Taurus. This Moon phase occurs at 1.42 UTC.

February 9 - Full Moon in Leo, Supermoon.

The Moon is on the opposite side of the Earth as the Sun and will be fully illuminated. This phase occurs at 7:33 UTC. This full moon is known as the Full Snow Moon because the heaviest snows usually fall during this month. Since hunting is difficult, this full moon has also been recognized as the Full Hunger Moon, since the harsh weather made fishing difficult. This is the first of four supermoons for 2020. The Moon will be at its nearest approach to the Earth and will look slightly larger and brighter than usual.

February 10 - Mercury at largest Eastern Elongation.

The planet Mercury reaches an eastern elongation of 18.1 degrees from the Sun.

February 15 – Last Quarter Moon in Scorpio.

This Moon phase occurs at 22.17 UTC.

February 18 – Mercury Retrograde begins in Pisces.

During a retrograde period, it isn't the right time to move forward in any practical venture. Be prepared for misunderstandings and miscommunications to be prevalent.

February 23 - New Moon in Aquarius.

The Moon is on the same side of the Earth as the Sun and will not be visible in the night sky. This phase occurs at 15:32 UTC. This is an excellent time to view galaxies and stars as there is no moonlight to obscure your view of the universe.

FEBRUARY WEEK ONE

This is the beginning of a new journey, your insight and ideas have created an environment which allows a new direction to be born. You can experience excellent outcomes on this journey. Cultivating your creative imagination, harnessing the power of flexibility, provides you with a gateway towards success. Your sensitivity and emotional awareness are guiding this process. Setting positive intentions lets you focus on important goals, opportunities arrive to support a phase of new growth. A milestone is soon reached which helps you map out future goals. Dreaming significant about the potential possible, you set your sights on targets which are lofty and substantial. You are ready to flex your winnings and gain traction on your aspirations. Focusing on the steps necessary paves the way for your dreams and goals to come into focus. A new era is sparked, developing this potential to nurtures your ideas. An important chapter emerges which lets you gain a glimpse of the robust results possible in your situation.

An important message crosses your path, an opportunity to network in a social environment provides you with emerging friendships. Happy news reaches you which brings blessings into your life. It is a cause for celebration, and this leaves you feeling optimistic. Abundance flows into your situation, and you can invest in expanding your horizons and taking on new areas which inspire you creatively. Valuable rewards are on offer, opening your mind and heart towards new situations brings a refreshing sense of freedom.

FEBRUARY WEEK TWO

The February 9th Supermoon flows a river of heightened potential into your sphere. This is the week which is richly abundant and combines special cosmic forces with divine vibrations. You will be able to take advantage of heightened opportunities which light an enticing path forward. New information reaches you to inspire your soul. It is a time of inspirational ideas and heart-to-heart communications which can create a shift towards setting essential goals.

Consequently, you are ready to expand your vision and take in a new area which begs to be developed. The reassessment of current priorities allows you to streamline your situation. This further solidifies your foundation and establishes an environment which is ripe for blossoming into a new area. You can create a substantial base, and this can be harnessed to further improve your bottom line. Security is heightened during this exciting phase, and this draws a happy situation into your life. Things are looking rosy, your hard work and perseverance let you achieve fantastic growth and abundance. Well-being and joy is the foundational basis of the changes you manifest.

You can ramp up the potential in your life, a festive vibration resonates warmly with your relaxed outlook. This ambiance is rejuvenating, it has positive effects on your well-being. You look forward to a harvest of abundance, seeds which have been planted are nourished and create positive outcomes for you. Significant changes ahead let you reveal stunning options. It is a golden time, which suggests positive news is imminent and can be utilized to expand your goals.

FEBRUARY WEEK THREE

You may be faced with a sense of restriction, conflict, or other disruption. A negative atmosphere which is limiting your energy may affect your spirit. Mercury retrograde which began on February 18th is up to its old tricks. Disagreements and miscommunication can negatively impact your environment. Faced with this troublesome energy, you can feed the agitation or stay mindful of the more important theme which is flowing through this phase. It can feel like a dark and testing time with a solution which is elusive, ambiguous and chaotic. If you focus on the situation too intensely, it becomes more tumultuous and risks spiraling out of control. Taking a step back and employing emotional empathy creates a channel for your dreams, imagination, and inspiration to flow. A river of healing soon arrives which absorbs the negativity. Understanding the quintessence beneath Mercury's troublesome vibrations paves the way for healing vibrations to reach your soul. An introspective shift clears the decks and enables you to resolve sensitivities. The stress you deal with under challenging conditions has been building, creating a healing sanctuary clears up a great deal of baggage which has been a burden on your spirit recently. Reflecting on the broader issues which have held your progress back does enable you to reach a turning point, a breakthrough provides a valuable gateway towards a chapter which gives you with gifts which nourish your soul. This helps you restore balance and replenishes your spirit. Surrendering to this process takes flexibility and patience, it draws beautiful healing moments, and ultimately, leads to new growth. Dealing with issues which have been brewing in the background of your life, take you towards a chapter which sees you ready to emerge and face the sun with a flourish.

FEBRUARY WEEK FOUR

You reach a crossroads where you find there is a need to make a sound decision. This suggests you are preparing to start a dynamic new cycle. Pressing forwards towards obtaining your aspirations enables you to take the initiative and be proactive about developing this potential. A significant outcome is indicated for those who express confidence and determination. A considerable change is available for you, the power of strength is coming into your life to assist you in creating this major shift. You may be anxious that life is about to get complicated, doing your homework will facilitate this process. If you have been struggling with uncertainty and confusion, you will resolve these fears. As you expand your boundaries, you discover that limitations are merely a mindset that hasn't been fully liberated. You are more than capable of breaking free of constraints and diving into uncharted territory. A desire to create a higher result will propel you forward towards your dreams, this leads to a sense of freedom which is exhilarating. You are gifted with strength and concentration this week, this meticulous attention to detail enables you to remove stumbling blocks and overcome issues. You learn to integrate your instincts with your analytical approach. This sees you making great strides, navigating forward towards achieving a new level of potential.

Additionally, an opportunity arrives to let your hair down with a more full social circle, this brings a great sense of fun and adventure into your life. It provides you with the right touch of balance between work and play.

MARCH ASTROLOGY

March 2 – First Quarter Moon in Gemini.

This Moon phase occurs at 19.57 UTC.

March 9 - Full Moon in Virgo, Supermoon.

This full Moon is on the opposite side of the Earth as the Sun and shall be fully illuminated. This phase occurs at 17:48 UTC. This full moon is known as the Full Worm Moon because this was the time of year when the ground would soften, and earthworms would reappear. This full moon is also known as the Full Crow Moon, the Full Crust Moon, the Full Sap Moon, and the Lenten Moon. This is also the last of four super-moons for 2020. The Moon will be closer to the Earth and will look slightly larger and brighter than usual.

March 9 - Mercury Retrograde ends in Aquarius.

You can now move forward with any delayed plans that you have been putting off due to the Mercury Retrograde phase. Relationships should soon improve as miscommunications are overcome

March 16 – Last Quarter Moon in Sagittarius.

This Moon phase occurs at 9.34 UTC. –

March 20 - March Equinox.

The March equinox takes place at 3:50 UTC. The Sun be shining on the equator, and there will be equal amounts of day and night throughout the world. This is the first day of spring (vernal equinox) in the Northern Hemisphere.

March 24 - New Moon in Aries.

The Moon is on the same side of the Earth as the Sun and will not be visible in the night sky. This phase occurs at 9:28 UTC. This is an excellent time to observe galaxies and stars because there is no moonlight to interfere.

March 24 - Mercury at most substantial Western Elongation.

The planet Mercury reaches its most substantial western elongation of 27.8 degrees from the Sun.

March 24 - Venus at most substantial Eastern Elongation.

The planet Venus reaches its most substantial Eastern elongation of 46.1 degrees from the Sun.

MARCH WEEK ONE

Revamping plans may be required, eliminating as much chaos from this process as possible will keep your potential heightened. Your determination and willpower matches your resourcefulness and leads you forward. You are in the midst of an intensely insightful transformation, mystical energy is providing a mystery element which has you delving deep. You explore an intriguing avenue, which sparks your curiosity. This would lead to a cycle which offers you substantial benefits, the biggest obstacle are the limitations in your own mind. Releasing pessimism, adopting a proactive and optimistic mindset is going to pay dividends. It allows you to harness the power of your thoughts and this culminates in a cycle which is packed with potential. You highlight a lucrative area which leads towards a creative venture, this sparks your artistic side. You're willing to work hard and establish yourself in a field which offers you security, happiness, and progression. The more you delve into this critical arena, the higher your talents evolve. It put you in contact with a broader range of people, this helps guide you towards continuing to develop this enticing path.

MARCH WEEK TWO

You focus on ideas which inspire you to begin developing a situation which motivates you to create growth. Your thoughts are highly creative, blending ideas and being flexible, forms a stable path forward. Your insight and planning allow you to create a valuable blueprint. You can feel anxious about creating a shift which does shakeup your environment. The changes ahead feel disconcerting but necessary. This uneasy feeling is building the ability for growth to occur. Navigating towards an uncertain future does feel emotionally uncomfortable. Acknowledging your feelings helps release anxiety, it puts you in a position where you balance your heart and mind and can let go of limiting patterns which halt progress. Persevering on your quest rewards you with a passage towards successful growth. Your natural resilience and resourcefulness may be put to the test, but you are well equipped to overcome hurdles and find the rewards which beckon you towards change. You plot a course using straightforward and persistent action. Your quest remains steadfast as you are determined to drive your situation forward. This is a time which is busy and enjoyable, your skills line up beautifully with an area which offers tangible rewards. You bring consistency into this environment, a burst of motivation heightens your productivity and draws stability into your situation. Creating a solid base from which to progress your vision is at the basis of this hard-working phase.

MARCH WEEK THREE

This is a phase which concentrates on having to surrender to waiting it out. You may feel a sense of restriction which limits your progress, or an unwillingness to move in a direction which you know is it necessary for you. You can take advantage of this holding pattern by creating the right environment which enables you to heal old wounds. It is in this therapeutic environment that you can resolve old areas which have caused you consternation and sadness. Dealing with the past can bring up raw emotions, the very fact that this does trigger you indicates there is healing work to be done before you are ready to embrace a new chapter of potential. It's not necessary to rush this process, healing is not a linear projection, it is something which occurs over time. Forgiveness and empathy, primarily when directed inward, can alleviate some of the stress of having to make progress or having to move forward to suit others expectations. Your situation is unique, you will know when it's the right time for you to start a new chapter.

Your friends become a stabilizing influence over the coming weeks, sharing of thoughts and ideas allows you to create compelling visions. Prioritizing your needs enables you to enliven your life, as you put your energy towards the areas which hold the most significant meaning. Enhance productivity also allows fast growth to inspire you further.

MARCH WEEK FOUR

The challenges of the past could trigger sensitivities, as you have been through some significant trials. Coming up with a solution for future goals, helps decode the puzzle, which currently holds you back. You do see improvements this week which tantalize you and tempt you to keep persevering towards your end goals. A surge of growth is possible which enables this area to improve exponentially through the care and dedication you apply to achieve your highest result. It can feel tedious, laborious, and extensive, not an accessible path, but one which offers you material rewards over time. Your innovative ideas align sweetly with a long term projection of success. Projects, productivity, and success are streaming you forward towards the realization of a bold enterprise. Making a firm move ahead, you are inspired to plan, and project visualized outcomes. A flight of fancy has you dreaming significant about the potential possible, your lofty goals encourage you to face challenges head-on and get your hands on a robust agenda. It is a time of determination and hard work, which leads to a new venture.

A signpost arrives which provides you with the gateway to happiness you have been yearning for. This beautifully aligns you towards a direction filled with creativity and inspiration. You turn a corner and upgrade your situation in a big way. Focusing on the essentials brings you towards building the right foundations needed for this to blossom.

APRIL ASTROLOGY

April 1 – First Quarter Moon in Cancer.

This Moon phase occurs at 10.21 UTC.

April 8 - Full Moon in Libra, Supermoon.

The Moon is on the opposite side of the Earth as the Sun and will be completely illuminated. This moon phase occurs at 2:35 UTC. This full moon is known as Full Pink Moon because it marked an appearance of the first spring flowers. This full moon has also been identified as the Sprouting Grass Moon, the Growing Moon, and the Egg Moon. Many coastal areas call it Full Fish Moon because this was the time the fish swam upriver to breed.

April 14 – Last Quarter Moon in Capricorn.

This Moon phase occurs at 22.56 UTC.

April 22, 23 - Lyrids Meteor Shower.

The Lyrids meteor shower runs each year from April 16-25. This meteor shower peaks on the night of the 22nd and the morning of the 23rd. These meteors sometimes produce bright dust trails that last for several seconds.

April 23 - New Moon in Taurus.

The New Moon is on the same side of the Earth as the Sun and will not be visible in the night sky. This moon phase occurs at 2:26 UTC. This is an excellent time to observe galaxies and stars because there is no moonlight visible.

April 30 – First Quarter Moon in Leo.

This Moon phase occurs at 20.38 UTC.

APRIL WEEK ONE

Fortune is shining upon you. This is a transition towards a significant event which is generally positive, it tends to collect the energy of other elements which surround you. You can expect developments to arise soon which give you a clearer understanding of the potential possible. As your fortune turns towards the sunnier skies, you face an auspicious chapter which provides you with added bonuses to improve your situation. It leads to a breakthrough which brings you towards a change that sets your dreams in motion. An opportunity ahead enables you to launch towards an area which offers progression. It is a time of developing substantial goals and diverging from your everyday circumstances. You can increase the potential by creating significant plans. In fact, a cycle of expansion is in motion for you. This takes you towards and abundant phase of heightened opportunity. Highly creative, you can harness this time to your advantage, and make progress towards advancing your dreams. You enter an ambitious phase, which plays a pivotal role in increasing your bottom line. Developments arise which tempt you towards a larger cycle of growth. A leadership role may be on offer, taking the bull by the horns, you dive into an opportunity which hones your talents and provides you with ample room for progression. Advancement is highlighted as being one of your priorities. This invites a serious offer, and you explore an intriguing opportunity which looks perfect for your vision. As you open a new door, you kick off a chapter which is exciting and bodacious.

APRIL WEEK TWO

There is an extraordinary opportunity to share your unique talents with another. This expression of your personal vision does help blend ideas together. You get valuable feedback into your insights. It is a productive chapter, which allows the opportunity to come knocking. Your unique vision and ability to pursue your goals with a laser beam focus clears the path ahead. You pinpoint areas which offer progression with a high degree of accuracy. You focus your energy on obtaining advancement. Cultivating your gifts provides you with talents which are set to flourish. There is terrific potential for fulfillment and social engagement, opportunities to mingle and network make themselves known to you during this time. You are intrepid and able to undercover uncover hidden leads, as you nurture a theme which undoubtedly serves your higher purpose. Research orientated excursion ticks all the boxes and enables you to plan thoughtfully for the future. It helps you develop a solid sense of what you can achieve shortly. Your unique combination of vision and practicality creates the alchemy of manifestation which is highly attuned towards a successful outcome. Your well thought out theories and practical application of ideas offer you a high level of achievement, fulfillment, and happiness. It allows you to advance your goalposts and discover a higher level of potential.

APRIL WEEK THREE

Progression is indicated, while it may not arrive as swiftly as you anticipated, you do benefit from increased security. This rewards you with a sense of stability, it enables you to plot a course towards achieving growth over time. You have plenty of energy and motivation to make the most of your strategic goals. This lets you focus on attaining headway on a venture which shows plenty of promise. This could even lead you in an entrepreneurial direction, and as you advance your interests, you start to revamp what is possible in your situation. You don't have to jump into anything without doing the due diligence necessary to make sure your projection is going to hold water. Focusing on preparing to take a big leap forward filters out distractions, and helps you sort through your priorities. Once you clarify your vision, you enter a highly productive time which is ripe for expansion. You are preparing for your next big venture, and there are power and strength within you during this time. A cluster of activity is coming your way, this shakes up your environment and creates a hot-spot of potential. Spending time contemplating your options is going to result in remarkable insights which enable you to plan for substantial goals. It also has the dual effect of fortifying your foundations and creating a strong sense of balance from which to propel forward. You are ready to benefit from events on the horizon, patience is necessary, as you gather your resources first and prepare to journey forwards.

APRIL WEEK FOUR

You find yourself in an area which leaves you feeling emotional, it is natural to crave a healing environment at moments which involve closing a chapter and preparing to enter a new path. You may be feeling a little out of your comfort zone and crave more introspection than usual. Giving yourself space you need to prepare for the season ahead, help you tap into your spiritual side. As your soul is soothed during this time, you pave the way for a new beginning to transition you forward. It's the perfect chance to release an area which has limited your progress. Healing resentful feelings release toxic energy which has burdened your spirit. Breaking free from the past, you can light up a new area of abundance to explore. This revamps your emotional awareness and leads to the development of a tempting area. Staying focused on self-development does help smooth over any rough edges during this transitional time. It restores your spirit and motivates you to focus on exploring your own dreams. This is a time where it is beneficial to pause and take stock of where you have come from and what you hope to achieve. The essence of pausing to reflect on your journey helps re-balance and restore equilibrium. It enables you to refine your goals and spotlight areas which may need to be adjusted. You need this sense of balance to ensure that you are heading in the right direction before you invest any more time and energy into this area. Checking in with your intuition provides that you can commit a hundred percent towards developing this path. Once you feel confident about the results possible, you get back to the process of turning your dreams into reality. It leads your practical side to make the necessary plans and create the steps needed to obtain a successful result.

May 6, 7 - Eta Aquarids Meteor Shower.

The Eta Aquarids meteor shower runs annually from April 19 to May 28. It peaks this year on the night of May 6 and the morning of May 7.

May 7 - Full Moon in Scorpio, Supermoon.

The Moon is on the opposite side of the Earth as the Sun, and its face will be fully illuminated. This phase occurs at 10:45 UTC. The May full moon is known as the Full Flower Moon because this was the time of year when spring flowers are in abundance. This full moon is also known as the Full Corn Planting Moon and the Milk Moon. This is also the last of four supermoons for 2020. The Moon will be at its closest approach to the Earth and looks slightly larger and brighter.

May 14 – Last Quarter Moon in Aquarius.

This Moon phase occurs at 14.03 UTC.

May 22 - New Moon in Taurus.

The Moon will be located on the same side of the Earth as the Sun and won't be seen in the night sky. This phase occurs at 17:39 UTC. The new moon phase is a brilliant time to observe galaxies and stars because there is no moonlight visible.

May 30 – First Quarter Moon in Virgo.

This Moon phase occurs at 3.30 UTC.

MAY WEEK ONE

This is an energizing time, the May 7th Supermoon leaves you feeling especially uplifted. Your motivation is a motivating force which has you feeling extra positive about future prospects. Some big news is arriving soon, which provides you with long-awaited feedback. A mentor offers you valuable support, and you get a sense of perspective about where your vision could take you. Revolutionary brainstorming sessions will lead to productive dialogues and lively conversations. It is an exact time, which offers valuable social engagement and helps you cultivate more time to spend with your tribe. This gives you an appropriate response from the daily slog of grinding your way to the top. You feel lighter and more connected with the entertaining areas of your life. The fires of creativity are smoldering, it is a highly flexible and innovative time which office you a real sense of being able to make progress in a creative area. Ultimately, this is leading you to develop an enterprise which is progressive and offers you the chance for growth. Things are coming together, it is a revitalizing chapter which takes you on a journey which stokes the artistic fires burning within. The underlying energy which simmers within your subconscious is seeking a creative avenue to express its potential. This brilliance provides fresh ideas which help support and nurture your potential. You make headway on developing key areas which help you achieve a result that matters.

MAY WEEK TWO

Golden movements this week open the floodgates to an auspicious phase. Progress swiftly occurs when you pour your focused energy into an area which is productive and rewarding. Significant potential spotlights the magic which is available during this breakthrough chapter. It provides you with an essential gateway towards improving the stability in your surroundings. Keeping your eye on business-related matters, you can embark on fine-tuning your goals and adding value to your situation. Constructive dialogues enable you to blend ideas with a valued mentor. This creates potent alchemy and helps you blaze towards the realization of your aspirations. You are ready to nurture a new area, information arrives, which is highly motivating. Your talents are prepared to flex their muscles in a direction which office you a chance for progression. Taking your abilities to a higher level enables your skills to grow. This facilitates a productive phase, which resonates warmly with your spirit, an excess of success is available utilizing the power of an optimistic outlook. Crossing over to this new path allows you to test the waters before diving deep into a situation which is on offer for someone with your expertise. It is a pivotal time where you can prioritize the achievement and advancement of your goals. Being proactive and diligent pays dividends as improvements quickly follow.

MAY WEEK THREE

Specific changes may trigger a sense of intensity. Adjusting to the surprises ahead help you forge through this time maintaining your sense of equilibrium. A few hurdles may test your patience, and this can drain your energy, ensuring that you can create space to gather support from your social sector, helps you maintain your course. Everything you set in motion does, in fact, grow and touch many areas of your life. As you reflect on the path ahead, you feel base with an area which is often neglected. Focusing on aligning your spirit towards the abundance which is seeking to make itself known to you, to provide you with a substantial way to draw a happier phase into being. Overcoming difficulties, you harness the power of your tenacious and resilient spirit. Your confidence in your abilities grows each time you overcome hurdles and find solutions to create a path towards your goals. You are ready to open the floodgates to a happier chapter. Shapeshifting towards an area which transforms your potential does let you embark on a green field of, particularly enticing potentiality. You get a glimpse of bold new waters which call your spirit. You are ready to break free of the holding pattern, which has limited your progress. As you loosen your grip on the shore, you are buoyed by an influx of opportunities which enable you to build momentum forward. A fresh perspective is imperative, this flexibility broadens your perception of what you are capable of. Taking the plunge into icy waters, you adopt a sink or swim approach which rewards you with swift progress. Fortune smiles upon your leap of faith, it activates hidden talents which emerge to support your growth. A venture you contribute towards draws significant attention, it builds into establishing yourself in an area which enables you to prosper further down the line.

MAY WEEK FOUR

This is a time of reflection, revision, and introspection. Pausing during this chapter enables you to make sure, it helps you deal with any unresolved feelings you may be having. It's a way to create space to deal with the emotional stress that could be affecting or impeding your progress. This is a pleasant time to plan for future contingencies allows you to move forward with a sustainable vision. Also, this enables you to connect with your core dreams and make sure it is still in alignment with your great purpose. You have a lofty goal in mind, which will do best with preparation and consideration before the big launch forward. Preparing your mindset before you dive in head first makes sure you have what it takes to get serious about achieving the steps necessary to succeed. Furthermore, a feasibility study will help determine whether your dreams are in alignment with available results.

Big changes ahead do indeed drive significant progress into your life. It enables a fresh start, which is in alignment with your emotional goals. Focusing on your priorities sparks a new era of potential. You can obtain stellar growth through harnessing the power of a compelling vision. This is a cathartic time which underscores an atmosphere of releasing outworn energy. Creating a clean slate energetically helps open the floodgates to a flow of potential which is ready to emerge. You can feel confident and hopeful about the future, you are being guided towards a destination which provides you with new potential.

June 4 - Mercury at Greatest Eastern Elongation.

The planet Mercury reaches greatest eastern elongation of 23.6 degrees from the Sun.

June 5 - Full Moon in Sagittarius.

The Full Moon is on the opposite side of the Earth as the Sun, and its face will be completely illuminated. This moon phase occurs at 19:12 UTC. This full moon is known as Full Strawberry Moon because it is the peak of the strawberry harvesting season. The June Full Moon has also been identified as the Full Rose Moon and the Full Honey Moon.

June 5 – Penumbral Lunar Eclipse.

This Moon eclipse occurs when the Moon passes through the Earth's partial shadow or penumbra. During this type of eclipse, the Moon will darken slightly but not completely disappear. This lunar eclipse will be visible throughout most of Europe, Africa, Asia, and Australia.

June 10 - Jupiter at Opposition.

The planet Jupiter will be at its nearest approach to Earth, and its planet face will be illuminated entirely by the Sun.

June 13 – Last Quarter Moon in Pisces.

This Moon phase occurs at 6.24 UTC.

June 17 – Mercury Retrograde begins in Cancer.

During a retrograde period, it isn't the right time to move forward in any practical venture. Be prepared for misunderstandings and miscommunications to be prevalent.

June 21 - June Solstice.

The June solstice occurs at 21:44 UTC. The North Pole will be tilted toward the Sun, which, having reached its northernmost position in the sky will be over the Tropic of Cancer at 23.44 degrees north latitude. This heralds the first day of summer (summer solstice) in the Northern Hemisphere, and is considered one of the most critical times of the year for many traditional cultures. It is the first day of winter (winter solstice) for the Southern Hemisphere.

June 21 - New Moon in Cancer.

The Moon is on the same side of the Earth as the Sun and will not be visible in the night sky. This moon phase occurs at 6:41 UTC. This is an excellent time to observe galaxies and stars because there is little moonlight to obstruct your view.

June 21 – Annual Solar Eclipse.

An annular solar eclipse occurs when the Moon is too far away from the Earth to completely cover the Sun. This results in a ring of light around the darkened Moon. The Sun's corona is not visible during an annular eclipse. The path of this solar eclipse begins in central Africa and travel through Saudi Arabia, northern India, and southern China before ending in the Pacific Ocean. A partial solar eclipse occurs throughout most of eastern Africa, the Middle East, and South Asia.

June 28 – First Quarter Moon in Libra.

This Moon phase occurs at 8.16 UTC.

JUNE WEEK ONE

You are the recipient of gifts during this fortuitous phase. It places you in the box seat to set your aspirations in motion. Your creativity expands all it touches, goals grow more substantial, and you are well positioned to improve your circumstances. You also balance this expansion with a reflective moment or two. This hits a sweet spot as it enables you to be mindful of maintaining a sense of balance and it allows you to touch base and refine your vision. An event on the horizon triggers surprise information. This news reaches you at precisely the right time, it turns into a source of fortune. This gives you a wonderful sense of confidence as you prepare to move ahead with your plans. You begin a dynamic and new cycle, which inspires you to focus on developing your goals. Pressing forward on your broader agenda creates an initiative which enables you to obtain progress. This advancement is your ticket for heightened motivation and productivity. It is a sweet chapter filled with friendship and a chance to mingle with your social set. You benefit from added support as your social life swings into high gear. It is a relaxing time, which brings you a heightened sense of well-being.

Additionally, you find this influence, one of expansion as you broaden your horizons. You get to explore new areas and form new connections with others socially. It is a time of personal growth, and the bonus is the effect it has on your confidence levels. Being open to new introductions diversely opens your life, and this proves to be a breath of fresh air for your spirit.

JUNE WEEK TWO

The planet Jupiter reaches its closest approach to the earth this week. It will be at its brightest, and this illuminates a new direction. Jupiters influence is one of luck, expansion and good fortune. You are leading up to a time which enables you to initiate an endeavor which holds promise. Upgrading your situation with an inspiring new plan, you head around a corner and can develop your circumstances in alignment with your passion. This leads to a healthful chapter which resonates warmly with your spirit. Great results are achieved through your willingness to sidestep hurdles and find solutions to any issues which hinder your progress. Breakthroughs are soon accomplished, and the pace is swift to follow. Your creative fires burn brightly as you touch on the area which is progressive and innovative. Your motivation provides you with the extra push required to step out of your comfort zone and mobilize your talents to achieve tangible results. Surprising news leads to an enticing offer, this gives you the chance to evolve to a new level of potential. Nurturing your gifts enables core talents to blossom, and this heralds an exciting chapter, which is inspiring and trailblazing. This leads to a phase which helps you drive your skills forward, it sets off a new cycle which you can develop over the coming months.

JUNE WEEK THREE

The June 21ˢᵗ Solstice merges serendipitously with an opportunity with your career. Revolutionary ideas arrive to support the goals you have in mind. You are dynamic and flexible, willing to streamline your objectives to obtain the highest result. This lets you carve out more time to develop a passion project. You shine a light on a nostalgic area which takes you back to the past. Long thought about dreams is allowed to progress. You enter a chapter which is growth orientated, restrictive patterns which have limited your potential are resolved, a theme of abundance shows up in your world and gets the ball rolling for you to head towards a happier chapter. As you advance your dreams, you pour your energy into an area which offers stunning potential. Putting the final touches on what you hope to achieve harnesses the element of air of manifestation, which supports your trajectory.

It is a pivotal time, which kicks off a bountiful cycle of auspicious growth. You accomplish a momentous achievement. As you advance your goals with a dynamic and tenacious outlook, the vibrancy you radiate encourages creative influences to flow freely. You can take advantage of an opportunity which captures your attention soon. This situation inspires your mind and tempts you to take proactive actions to achieve expansion.

JUNE WEEK FOUR

You generate leads which see an expansion of horizons. Embracing the changes ahead, you enter a time of developing your talents and learning new skills. This brings you in contact with other talented individuals. It leads to sharing thoughts and ideas and the creation of new forms. Your landscape is currently shifting, passion and adventure are tempting you towards creating a seismic shift which encourages a flow of new potential into your world. This has you thinking about the number of future possibilities. You discover an area which begs to be developed. As your creative juices flow, you experience a rash of inspired thought processes which enable you to develop some realistic plans to use as a steppingstone to your more ambitious goals.

Information is revealed, which sends your life on an upswing. You enter a fortuitous and auspicious chapter which provides you with the ability to transform your outlook and create significant change in your world. You walk a path, which is more in alignment with your personal vision. You explore options which bring out your positive side, and this leaves you feeling optimistic about the future. It is a critical phase which releases burdens and draws a sense of abundance into your world. You feel ablaze with new inspiration. Additionally, finding your more extensive spiritual tribe enables you to mingle with others who hold the same mindset. It leads to heightened opportunities for your social life as new activities crop up to be explored.

July 5 - Full Moon in Capricorn.

The July Full Moon is located on the opposite side of the Earth as the Sun and will be fully illuminated. This phase occurs at 4:44 UTC. This full moon is known as Full Buck Moon because the male buck deer start to grow new antlers. This full moon is also known as the Full Thunder Moon and the Full Hay Moon.

July 5 – Penumbral Lunar Eclipse.

This Moon eclipse occurs when the Moon passes through the Earth's partial shadow or penumbra. During this type of eclipse, the Moon will darken slightly but not completely disappear. This lunar eclipse will be visible throughout most of Europe, Africa, Asia, and Australia.

July 12 – Last Quarter Moon in Aries.

This Moon phase occurs at 23.29 UTC.

July 12 - Mercury Retrograde ends in Cancer.

You can now move forward with any delayed plans that you have been putting off due to the Mercury Retrograde phase. Relationships should soon improve as communication improves.

July 14 - Jupiter at Opposition.

The Giant planet Jupiter will be at its nearest approach to Earth and will be at it's brightest.

July 20 - New Moon in Cancer.

The July New Moon is located on the same side of the Earth as the Sun and won't be visible in the night sky. This moon phase occurs at 17:33 UTC. This is an excellent time to observe galaxies and stars because there is no moonlight visible.

July 20 - Saturn at Opposition.

The beautiful ringed planet Saturn will be at its nearest approach to Earth and will be illuminated by the Sun.

July 22 - Mercury at Greatest Western Elongation.

The planet Mercury reaches greatest western elongation of 20.1 degrees from the Sun.

July 27 – First Quarter Moon in Scorpio.

This Moon phase occurs at 12.32 UTC.

July 28, 29 - Delta Aquarids Meteor Shower.

The Delta Aquarids meteor shower peaks on the night of July 28 and morning of July 29. The first quarter moon may block many of the fainter meteors this year. You should still be able to view the brighter ones. Best viewing will be at a dark vista after midnight. Meteors radiate from the constellation Aquarius but can appear anywhere in the sky.

JULY HOROSCOPE

JULY WEEK ONE

You enter a time of intrigue, mystery and fanciful escape. New possibilities arise which spark your interest. This has the potential to create a shift which becomes a significant turning point for your spiritual growth. Revealing an original path you get in touch with a realm usually hidden below conscious awareness. It creates a life-affirming potential and begins a new chapter for you. You can plot a course towards revealing the truth, which lays beneath the surface of your awareness. Insight, introspection, and reflection create space to understand your higher purpose. This puts you in touch with a direction which speaks to your heart and is in alignment with your core vision.

This is a time which enables outstanding bonds to be rebalanced. There may be boundaries which need reestablishing, or other areas of your social life, which require more of your time and energy to nurture the potential possible. Any disrupted communications or ruffled feathers from Mercury retrograde's recent disturbance will be offset by the extra care you offer your personal relationships during this time. This kicks off a chapter which provides you with plenty of social connection and enables you to nurture the ties that count in your life. An event crops up, which allows you to celebrate with friends. You may find you are ready to level a personal situation, up to a more profound commitment. This takes you towards building a union that still enables you to keep your life but lets you enjoy more mutual time and shared experiences together.

JULY WEEK TWO

Mercury Retrograde ends on the 12th of July, and this sees you successfully emerge from a cocoon where you have sheltered your creativity recently. Breaking free you undergo a metamorphosis which takes you towards a more adventurous and creative chapter. It is an energizing time which allows you to grow your talents and dive into new areas. Your optimistic outlook maintains a forward flow of positivity which enhances your potential. A gateway of raw possibilities projects a phantasmagoria of options into your awareness. Sifting through the various options, you are struck by one area which appears significant. This is a signpost and exploring this avenue leads to positive change. You open your heart, soul, and mind to a new realm of exciting potential. You are determined to develop a grand idea, and there is strength in your spirit to follow through with the work required to create an ideal outcome.

As you begin the voyage forward, you have a sense of being able to focus on an area which holds meaning to you, and this brings you joy. This sees you head towards a direction which is in alignment with your higher vision. Sudden change brings you the opportunity which will allow you to break free of restrictions. Something is unfolding, you are being advised to be patient so that things can unfold in due course of time.

JULY WEEK THREE

This is an excellent time as it brings opportunities into your world. It lights up a sense of achievement and recognition. Following your heart enables you to reach your desired outcome. This also rewards you with more stability and self-sufficiency. As you become responsible for expanding into new areas of growth, you make a courageous decision which provides you with ample determination to succeed. You receive a boost from the information which flows back to you, this could come in the form of confidential feedback shared with another. Knowing that you are creating some waves allows you to get an idea of the impact you are having in your broader environment. Your focus is on security and how to create more wealth in your life. This heightens your power of manifestation, you are likely to transition to a new chapter which enables you to embark on a phase of increased growth opportunities. An exciting offer arrives to entice you into a valued area. Facing an important decision, you contemplate your options and plot a course towards an action driven environment. Your choices are based on a strategic plan, applying your keen analytical powers to this process puts you in the right context to succeed. Your ambitious plans seek realization in tangible form. Taking stock of potential obstacles, you visualize your outcomes and begin a practical chapter of turning your attention to the details of implementing your strategies.

JULY WEEK FOUR

You are ready to heal old wounds, clearing your energy and aligning your spirit towards healing enables you to resolve any residual issues which have been limiting your progress recently. It does pave the way for a regular practice of self-nurturing. Being mindful of the things which trigger your sensitivities shine a light on which areas are most problematic for you. This begins the process of resolving old issues and building foundations which enable you to feel more emotionally secure. This gives you a basis of grounded energy from which to create a strong sense of well-being as your foundation. You reach a crossroads which see you face a sense of uncertainty. Knowing which path to take, will be extremely beneficial but does require an understanding of contemplation, doing the mental work necessary enables you to choose wisely and follow through on your decision. Preparing for a new journey allows you to move forward and illuminate the available magic. You are ready for adventure and movement. This life transition is prepared to take you towards a highly creative phase. Exciting developments soon motivate you to keep expanding your horizons. An infusion of creative energy ignites new potential in your life. Progress is coming, and this does draw an exciting phase, which leads to an emotionally fulfilling journey.

AUGUST ASTROLOGY

August 3 - Full Moon in Aquarius.

The August Full Moon is located on the opposite side of the Earth as the Sun and will be fully illuminated. This phase occurs at 15:59 UTC. The August full moon is known as the Full Sturgeon Moon because sturgeon fish of the Great Lakes and other major lakes were quickly caught during this time. This full moon has also been known as the Green Corn Moon and the Grain Moon.

August 11 – Last Quarter Moon in Taurus.

This Moon phase occurs at 16.45 UTC.

August 12, 13 - Perseids Meteor Shower.

The Perseids meteor shower runs each year from July 17 to August 24. It peaks this year on the night of August 12 and the morning of August 13. The Perseids meteor shower is one of the best to view as the meteors are so bright and numerous. The best viewing is from a dark vista after midnight.

August 13 - Venus at Greatest Western Elongation.

The planet Venus reaches greatest western elongation of 45.8 degrees from the Sun.

August 19 - New Moon in Leo.

The Moon will be on the same side of the Earth as the Sun and will not be visible in the night sky. This moon phase occurs at 2:41 UTC. This is an excellent time to observe galaxies and stars because there is no moonlight to obstruct the view.

August 25 – First Quarter Moon in Scorpio.

This Moon phase occurs at 17.58 UTC.

AUGUST WEEK ONE

You enter a busy time, which begins a new chapter. A newfound sense of confidence and clarity pave the way towards developing your goals. You transform towards a lighter section, which is focused on improving stability and security. Working towards your aspirations, you find yourself in a productive environment. It's the perfect time to generate new leads and obtain positive results. A stable platform is built through the dedication and focused attention you apply to improve your circumstances. While things may not progress as quickly as you would like, you are entering a phase which enables you to plot a course towards achieving robust growth. Prioritizing your energy pays dividends, it takes you towards creating an environment which offers healthy rewards. You begin to see a path inviting you forwards towards the achievement of goals and the attainment of happiness. Making strides towards your dreams. You exhibit a willingness to put yourself in new environments and learn new areas during this active phase.

AUGUST WEEK TWO

This is a time of repose where you may be forced to await developments outside of your control. It can feel unsettling and does require patience as information will be revealed in due course. Re-balancing your mind, calming your emotions is essential to maintaining equilibrium. Just taking time to be mindful and present at the moment helps you deal with any unsettling vibrations which could be affecting your spirit. Pausing and reflecting on the path ahead enables valuable insight into your current situation. Ripples of awareness resonate throughout this phase, allowing you to see the bigger picture. It is also the perfect opportunity to embrace forgiveness, closure, and endings. Creating space to heal what has gone before, does in fact, liberate your soul. This ultimately leads to a new chapter of potentiality. You are self-sufficient and independent, capable as you ride out any emotional turbulence and prepare to set sail towards smoother waters.

Discussing your thoughts with a valued mentor helps to bounce your ideas around with someone who provides you with valuable insight into the path ahead. You gain an idea of what may be possible in your situation and this encourages you to can continue to explore your options and map out a path which leads you towards your dreams. You are adventurous and harness a trailblazing spirit to accomplish your ambitious goals. It is a time of discovery and expansion, a willingness to open your mind and heart to new environments pays dividends.

AUGUST WEEK THREE

Your powers of sound visualization and manifestation hold you in good stead. Luck and motivation arrive to tempt you towards a new phase. You are flexible and adaptable, able to discern which direction to head towards. You are highly attuned towards improving your circumstances, your intuition is a guiding light which lets you gain clarity into your higher calling. You may find your priorities shift during this time, necessary changes are coming, and your vision is streamlined to create an environment conducive to substantial growth. You usher in the chapter, which is highly creative and attracts new potential into your world. There is a sense of synchronicity around the changes which follow, it is an exact time which sees advancement occurring in critical areas of your life. You may notice a signpost which points you in a direction previously unseen. This is to drive you forward towards learning a diverse field which may, in turn, inspire you in ways you hadn't anticipated. It is a continuum of growth and advancement, which in turn motivates and encourages you to make the most of your abilities.

AUGUST WEEK FOUR

You enter a valuable chapter which offers you the ability to release baggage which has weighed heavily on your shoulders for some time. A rush of lightness soon follows this emotional release. Doing cathartic inner work may trigger sensitivities, yet it does create space for healing. You improve your circumstances through your willingness to overcome hurdles and open your mind to try out new modalities which can assist you on your journey of self-development. Learning new areas paves the way for inspiration to arrive to tempt you towards a lively chapter of growth. Your innovative ideas lead to a grand reveal when you unleash your talents and focus on developing a game-changing endeavor. This essential chapter points to a breakthrough moment which shines a light on advancement. Finding your groove. Let's your vision come together nicely. It can lead to rapid growth so preparing for significant changes help to stabilize your situation during the phase ahead. It is an adventurous chapter which nurtures your emotion while increasing the options available to you. You feel creatively inspired to dive deep and begin a new section.

September 2 - Full Moon in Pisces.

The September full Moon is on the opposite side of the Earth as the Sun, and its face will be fully illuminated. This phase occurs at 5:22 UTC. This full moon is known as the Full Corn Moon because the corn is harvested around this time.

September 10 – Last Quarter Moon in Gemini.

This Moon phase occurs at 9.26 UTC.

September 11 - Neptune at Opposition.

The giant blue planet will be at its closest approach to Earth, and its face will be illuminated by the Sun.

September 17 - New Moon in Virgo.

The Moon is on the same side of the Earth as the Sun and will not be visible in the night sky. This phase occurs at 11:00 UTC. This is an excellent time to observe galaxies and stars because there is no moonlight visible.

September 22 - September Equinox.

The 2020 September equinox occurs at 13:31 UTC. The Sun shines directly on the equator, creating equal amounts of day and night throughout the world. This is also the first day of fall (autumnal equinox) in the northern hemisphere and is considered a significant zodiac event for many traditional cultures.

September 24 – First Quarter Moon in Capricorn.

This Moon phase occurs at 1.55 UTC.

SEPTEMBER HOROSCOPE

SEPTEMBER WEEK ONE

Positive changes arrive and tempt you to direct your excess energy into a channel which is expansive and transformational. Opening a gateway towards growth, you create a shift which guides you towards a happier future. New goals and dreams emerge, you are submerged in a broader landscape of what is possible for your life. The future is paved with hidden gems which sparkle with potential. Your optimistic outlook embraces new challenges, are you knuckle down to the business of working hard and stoking the fires of your creative spirit. You benefit from the information which is revealed to you soon. This sign gives you the chance to move your goals forward, it is an emotionally rewarding time, you balance your emotions with aspirations, and channel your creativity into developing a situation which holds value in your life. Finding your real purpose provides you with a strong foundation, it becomes the basis from which to propel your dreams forward. You see a broader pattern forming of the direction your life is leading you. It is a time which beckons with potential and you are inspired by the changes ahead. Your life burns brightly with new opportunities which fire up your imagination. The excitement and adventure figure prominently over the subsequent phase. You are also able to release an area which has been problematic recently and limited your progress. This leads to creating an environment which is empowering and sees you thrive under the flow of abundance which streams into the situation.

SEPTEMBER WEEK TWO

The planet Neptune is at its closest approach to Earth this week, it will be at its brightest. Neptune rules your house of dreams and healing. This is a time of pausing and reflecting on your goals, fine-tuning is required to streamline the process as scattering your energy into many directions is having a detrimental effect on advancing your aspirations. Letting go of areas which haven't reached their true potential clears the path for you to make positive change. Trusting in your intuition to guide your way forward takes you further than previously imagined. You can set appropriate boundaries and still garner respect from those you value. It is a beneficial time to create space to focus on self-development, paying attention to your needs, enables you to harness a force of strength and determination. A time of rejuvenation leads towards a chapter which offers many blessings. You power through the opportunities which cross your path, releasing outworn energy, rebalancing, frayed emotions. You are willing to do the work needed to improve your circumstances. There is also support available in your broader social circle which draws a strong sense of connection into your world. It is a foundation built on solid bonds and a stable environment. You transition towards a chapter which resonates positively with your spirit. As you unlock the key to a new episode of potential, you gain insight into the potential possible in your world.

SEPTEMBER WEEK THREE

You complete a cycle, and this has you wondering what direction to head in the next. You do best when kept busy and productive, evaluating your mission does take you towards learning a new skill which complements your current talents. This guides you forward towards a phase which offers many gifts and blessings. As you transition towards a new area, you prepare to plan and map out developing a pet project, which is close to your heart. Options are revealed which inspire your mind and this motivates you to plan ambitiously for a bodacious vision which sees you reaching for your dreams. You get back to the process of reevaluation and revision. Refining your goals leads to sifting through old emotions, tying up loose ends, and creating space to improve your vision. It can be a complicated process as you may need to let go of an area which you had been focusing on. Tearing down outworn energy creates the effect of rejuvenating your potential. Ultimately, you are headed towards renewal, this clears the decks and creates an environment ripe for an influx of new possibility. Soon after you prepare to ignite your inspiration on a new endeavor which makes itself known to you.

SEPTEMBER WEEK FOUR

The Equinox this week indicates growth opportunities arriving in the form of a chance which is worthy of exploring. You delight in the changes which occurred during this exciting time. Emerging from quiet time in your life, you are ready to seek new adventures. Social invitations bring you in contact with inspiring people who understand your thoughts and offer you their own pearls of wisdom. This puts a smile on your face, you embrace a more social vibe and can enjoy, having fun with like-minded individuals. A sense of freedom surrounds your awareness, you break free of restrictions and let your hair down in a relaxed environment. It is a time of developing social bonds and enjoying life. An opportunity crops up, which offers you a wild path of creative abandon. You can set yourself free in an area which inspires you to be flamboyant and express your artistic side. This opens a new phase of potential, inspiration is heightened, allowing you to set your sights on an important goal. It is a time which sees an influx of powerful energy, ramp up your spirit. Revolutionizing and expanding your horizons creates an impulsive shift, and this is guiding you towards discovering new adventures. You make headway on a personal goal which holds meaning to you. The significance of this development underscores a theme of abundance emerging in your situation. This puts an optimistic tinge on the events which follow.

October 1 - Full Moon in Aries.

The October full Moon is on the opposite side of the Earth as the Sun, and its face will be fully illuminated. This phase occurs at 21:05 UTC. This full moon is known as the Hunters Moon because at this time of year the leaves are falling, and the game is ready. This full moon is also known as the Travel Moon and the Blood Moon. This moon is also known as the Harvest Moon. The Harvest Moon is the full moon that occurs closest to the September equinox each year.

October 1 - Mercury at Greatest Eastern Elongation.

The planet Mercury reaches greatest eastern elongation of 25.8 degrees from the Sun.

October 7 - Draconids Meteor Shower.

The Draconids meteor shower runs annually from October 6-10 and peaks this year on the night of the 7th.

October 10 – Last Quarter Moon in Cancer.

This Moon phase occurs at 0.39 UTC.

October 13 – Mercury Retrograde begins in Scorpio.

During a retrograde period, it isn't the right time to move forward in any practical venture. Be prepared for misunderstandings and miscommunications to be more prevalent.

October 16 - New Moon in Libra.

The Moon will be on the same side of the Earth as the Sun and will not be seen in the night sky. This moon phase occurs at 19:31 UTC. This is an excellent time of the month to view galaxies and stars because there is no moonlight visible.

October 21, 22 - Orionids Meteor Shower.

The Orionids meteor shower runs yearly from October 2 to November 7. Orionids meteor shower peaks this year on the night of October 21 and the morning of October 22.

October 23 – First Quarter Moon in Capricorn.

This Moon phase occurs at 13.23 UTC.

October 31 - Full Moon, Blue Moon in Taurus.

The October full Blue Moon is on the opposite side of the Earth as the Sun, and its face will be fully illuminated. This phase occurs at 14:49 UTC. This is the second full moon in the same month, it is referred to as a blue moon.

October 31 - Uranus at Opposition.

The planet Uranus will be at its nearest approach to Earth, and its face will be illuminated by the Sun.

OCTOBER HOROSCOPE

OCTOBER WEEK ONE

Vitality and dynamic energy are at the crux of this phase. You are energetic, confident, and capable. You harness your creativity to produce substantial outcomes. There is an innovative element to this chapter which suggests you embark on a new endeavor which holds promise. It is a necessary time which sets your imagination free, listening to your gut feelings captures the essence of your intuition. You feel encouraged to keep developing an area which offers a robust potential. Carving out your own niche on a passion project, your inspiration is fueled by a desire to make a unique mark on the world. A firm decision is required to choose the path ahead. A fork in the road has created two options for you to consider. As you contemplate which direction to head towards, you receive valuable information which enables you to plot your trajectory safely. You think about long term implications as part of this process of choosing wisely. This is a situation which encourages decisive action, taking a courageous step forward is a proactive statement which boldly sets your intention and makes a mark on what is possible in your world. The air of manifestation is surrounding you and supporting your growth during this critical phase.

OCTOBER WEEK TWO

This is a time of rapid and sudden shifts which could destabilize your spirit. Raw emotions rise from the depths of your subconscious, creating space to resolve and heal troublesome feelings helps restore equilibrium. You are transitioning to a new phase of growth, but it also suggests that leaving something behind is the cause of this sense of melancholy. You plant the seeds of renewal and rejuvenation by making yourself a focus during this time. Nurturing your spirit at this time creates the right environment for you to blossom in the chapter ahead. Your vision gains momentum, you gain traction on obtaining a goal which offers you vibrant rewards. You are focused and determined, innovative, creative, and capable during this productive phase. Streamlining and organizing your priorities shift your focus forward, it creates the right environment for you to thrive and succeed in your endeavors. The winds of change sweep in to entice you to grow your talents and build foundations which are stable and progressive. There is a lot of activity coming into your life, developing your situations pay dividends in the physical realm as you can begin to see the tangible rewards arriving from the efforts you have extended.

OCTOBER WEEK THREE

A goal you've been working hard to complete finally comes together for you. The combination of this undertaking and the efforts dished out to reach this point, give you a bigger idea of what you can accomplish. This newly found confidence plays an essential role in the events which follow. Transitioning to a new venture wraps up the previous cycle and tempts you to distill the magic learned into a new area. The chemistry of manifestation surrounds you, your creativity is heightened, you are ready to plant the seeds for the next chapter. Your inspiration is reawakened, it's the perfect time to set your intentions and take action towards planning your goals. This is an adventurous time, which is all about revolution and reinvention. Courage and strength guide you forward towards testing the waters of a new path. It may feel like a leap of faith into the unknown, if things pan out as planned, you will gain a greater sense of security in the long run. Your finances and resources are set to benefit from the dedication and perseverance you apply to this journey.

OCTOBER WEEK FOUR

The planet Uranus will be at its closest approach to Earth this week. The planet Uranus rules the center of change and originality. You embark on an adventurous chapter which sees you relish new found freedom. Life picks up speed and offers you attractive opportunities for growth. This prompts you to open your heart to change, Championing for your passions leads to creative time which is uniquely empowering. Meeting new people along the way creates a turbocharged aspect which is highly enticing. This becomes a broadening influence which brings you a sense of diversity which is attractive. You sink your teeth into learning new areas and thrive in developing goals which spark your curiosity and ignite the creative side of your mind. Being open to these new adventures remarkably opens your life, this provides you with a breath of fresh air which cleanses the past and sweeps them to entice you to dream big about the future. This is a highly productive time, which has you focus on practical aspects. A deal is agreed upon, and decisions are made which further your cause. Your ability to organize and obtain high results does give you a significant advantage. It is a productive and grounding phase, which enables you to focus on your goals and set new and profitable priorities for growth. A whirlwind of exciting changes flows into your world. Transforming these discoveries into productive endeavors put you in the box seat to improve your circumstances. You build your potential from the ground up, a compelling opportunity arrives, which heightens the financial potential possible. Seeing the rewards flow in from the hard work you have been diligently outpouring unleashes a sense of abundance. It has an uplifting effect on your life, you feel independent and capable of achieving substantial goals.

November 3 - Mercury Retrograde ends in Libra.

You can now move forward with any delayed plans that you have been putting off due to the Mercury Retrograde phase. Relationships should soon improve as miscommunications resolve.

November 4, 5 - Taurids Meteor Shower.

The Taurids meteor shower runs yearly from September 7 to December 10. It peaks this year on the night of November 4.

November 8 – Last Quarter Moon in Leo.

This Moon phase occurs at 13.46 UTC.

November 15 - New Moon in Scorpio.

The Moon is on the same side of the Earth as the Sun and will not be visible in the night sky. This phase occurs at 5:07 UTC. This is an excellent time to view galaxies and star clusters because there is no moonlight visible.

November 17, 18 - Leonids Meteor Shower.

The Leonids meteor shower runs yearly from November 6-30. The Leonids meteor shower peaks this year on the night of the 17th and morning of the 18th.

November 22 – First Quarter Moon in Pisces.

This Moon phase occurs at 4.45 UTC.

November 30 - Full Moon in Gemini.

The November full Moon is on the opposite side of the Earth as the Sun, and its face will be fully illuminated. This phase occurs at 9:30 UTC. This full moon is known as Full Beaver Moon as this was the time of year to set beaver traps before the swamps and rivers froze. It is also known as the Frosty Moon and the Hunter's Moon.

November 30 - Penumbral Lunar Eclipse

A penumbral lunar eclipse occurs when the Moon passes through the Earth's partial shadow or penumbra. During this type of eclipse, the Moon will darken but not completely eclipse. This Penumbral lunar eclipse will be visible throughout most of North America, the Pacific Ocean, and northeastern Asia.

NOVEMBER HOROSCOPE

NOVEMBER WEEK ONE

You may feel overwhelmed by an environment which is chaotic and demanding. Multitasking and juggling too many situations and duties can leave you feeling frazzled. Being mindful that overreaching isn't going to get you there any more quickly. Learning to pull back and pace yourself provides you with a stable path through this busy phase. You can handle the demands on your time and delegating the task to others also allows you to streamline your situation and focus on your priorities. It is a time which shines a spotlight on expansion and entrepreneurial endeavors. You bring an essential project to completion, one which has special significance on your career path. Finishing a phase of growth that helps tie up a few loose ends brings you a welcome sense of recognition. Doing your personal best comes easy for you, you excel at setting goals and planning for your next big project. You may find you are the welcome recipient of a windfall, as luck and Fortune is surrounding you during this fortuitous time. It is a dominant phase which illuminates new potential and paves the way towards building a brighter future. Some of the heaviness of the past begins to lift, your mind is buzzing with new ideas and aspirations. Kicking back with kindred spirits also provides you with a broader audience to share your thoughts with. Conversations which focus on the development of entrepreneurial ideas are likely to plant the seeds for future growth.

NOVEMBER WEEK TWO

As you reflect on the changes which currently surround your life, you will have a more significant epiphany of how much you have accomplished on your journey so far. A flood of inspiration returns into your world, and this takes you to a vibrant chapter which heralds abundant potential arriving to expand your horizons. A new section is possible. This sees increasing stability occurring on your home front. Something you have been hoping for turns a corner and begins to show promise. This brings you to a happier phase and does provide you with the positive changes you have been needing. Trusting in your higher self and destiny is part of this process. Advancement is in the pipeline; you could get involved in a new initiative which provides you with a wealth of opportunities. You take advantage of heightened benefits for socializing. It brings a strong sense of balance into your personal life. Focusing on your tribe becomes a priority, this brings harmony into your world. This leads to potential being revealed which helps to heal old wounds. It is likely to be a chapter which provides you with lasting benefits. You discover you have the freedom in your life which can take you to a new level of possibility.

NOVEMBER WEEK THREE

You have accumulated a great deal of wisdom and fortitude. You may feel a sense of restriction in your life's journey at present; this is guiding you to obtain enlightenment, getting to the bottom of what your soul desires will see you focusing your energy on an area which holds promise. You reach a turning point soon, and this brings an ending, it also heralds significant changes occurring during this phase. You may find yourself offered an opportunity out of the blue, which dramatically opens new doorways. This is a beautiful time for self-development and beginning a practice of self-nurturing. This enables you to heal old wounds and builds the right foundations for future growth. This takes you to a buoyant chapter which inspires and motivates you to connect with like-minded individuals. You experience lively communications, and it does bring a valuable sense of harmony into your surroundings. Finding your synergistic groove, bring you fresh opportunities to mingle and communicate with fascinating characters. Liberating yourself from everyday constraints lets, you harness dynamic energy, as limitations are removed. Freedom and adventure await an open heart. New inspiration sweeps into your life, which in turn inspires you to move forward towards a new phase of potential. Personal growth is a significant aspect of this path, it reveals a world which is dynamic, harmonious, and abundant.

NOVEMBER WEEK FOUR

An invitation arrives to entice you to engage more with your social life. It leads to a winning time where you connect with others who energize and enliven your life. You discover that sharing resources with another leads to a chapter which offers many solutions. Your aspirations are guiding this process and heighten motivation arrives to keep things flowing forward. This is a grounded chapter which gives you a chance to express yourself fully. This does usher in expanded opportunities. It is an expansive month which highlights self-expression and creativity. Heightened social opportunities provide you with well-deserved opportunities to relax. It takes you towards building foundations which involve bonding, intimacy and merging of dreams. Your emotion runs strong but also your will to deepen the potential possible. The fun times are set to unfurl later this year, this light up areas of inspiration and adventure. You emerge from the confines which have limited progress in the past and reconnect with a broader world of potential.

December 8 – Last Quarter Moon in Virgo.

This Moon phase occurs at 0.37 UTC.

December 13, 14,15 - Geminids Meteor Shower.

The Geminids meteor shower runs each year from December 7-17. The Geminids meteor showers peaks this year on the night of the 13th, 14th, and 15th. The nearly new moon this year will provide dark skies for an excellent show. Best viewing will be from a dim vista after midnight. Meteors will radiate from the constellation Gemini but can appear anywhere in the sky.

December 14 - New Moon in Sagittarius.

The Moon is on the same side of the Earth as the Sun and will not be visible in the night sky. This moon phase occurs at 16:17 UTC. This is an excellent time to view galaxies and stars because there is no moonlight visible.

December 21 – First Quarter Moon in Pisces.

This Moon phase occurs at 23.41 UTC.

December 21 - December Solstice.

The 2020 December solstice occurs at 10:02 UTC. The South Pole of the earth tilts toward the Sun, which, having reached its most southern place in the sky, is directly over the Tropic of Capricorn at 23.44 degrees south latitude. This December solstice also marks the first day of winter (winter solstice) in the Northern Hemisphere.

December 21 – Great Conjunction of Jupiter and Saturn.

A conjunction of Jupiter and Saturn will take place on December 21. This is known as great conjunction as it is a rare celestial event. The last great conjunction occurred in the year 2000. The two bright planets will appear only 7 arc minutes of each other in the night sky. They will be so close that they will seem to make a bright double planet. Look to the west just after sunset for this impressive and rare planetary pair.

December 21, 22 - Ursids Meteor Shower.

The Ursids meteor shower occurs each year from December 17 - 25. This meteor event peaks this year on the night of the 21st and morning of the 22nd.

December 30 - Full Moon in Cancer.

The Moon is on the opposite side of the Earth as the Sun, and its face will be fully illuminated. This moon phase occurs at 03:28 UTC. This full moon is known as the Full Cold Moon because this is the time of year when the cold winters air arrives and nights become long and dark. This full moon is known as the Long Nights Moon and the Moon Before Yule.

DECEMBER WEEK ONE

You are going through a time of bringing up old emotions to resolve them so you can enter a fresh slate of potential. You reveal what has been hindering your progress, you reach a breakthrough point, allowing you to move forward towards an important goal. You are set to see improvements in your life with a phase which highlights self-expression and creativity. This takes you towards expanding your horizons, and it has a beautiful effect of releasing tension and restoring balance. You have made great tracks on your personal journey. This sees you continue to evolve towards achieving substantial growth and more excellent stability. A shift occurs which invites you to expand your horizons. You spend quality time with your closest family ties, and this connects you with a sense of grounded energy which is essential in this beginning this new area. You set your sights on achieving an excellent outcome, and nothing will deter you from your higher vision. Change is indicated. Sweeping changes are coming which revolutionizes your life. This reshuffles the decks of potential.

DECEMBER WEEK TWO

You may find your priorities have shifted recently, focus on your foundations first as notable changes are indicated. This is highlighted by fulfilling interactions with others. You accomplish a great deal by engaging with your broader social circle. Networking introduces positive influences into your world. You take a positive approach and align your energetic vibration with one who holds meaning to you. Life picks up the pace; there is a whirlwind of activity which leads to a hectic environment. This highlights a desire to gain more balance and harmony within your life. Taking matters into your own hands provides you with a trajectory which leads to expanding your horizons. This is a favorable time to upgrade your dreams and go after what you truly want. Your insights welcome in a productive phase, which is lively and allows your soul to flourish. Information arrives to help guide your objectives. This is a beautiful time to map a solid plan for future growth, the goals you set during this time are likely to provide you with tangible results over the coming months.

DECEMBER WEEK THREE

Surprise news arises, and this could be from someone you haven't heard from for a while. This beautifully orientates towards developing a bond which bolsters your mood. A relationship is set to blossom, and this sees you discussing the future potential with someone who holds meaning in your life. Choosing to act on developing this bond does place you in the box seat for future growth. Your life is on the upswing, and you enter a lucky and expansive time in your personal life. This provides you with the renewed energy to embark on a new chapter of potential. Your situation reveals a clear path; this takes you to an expansive cycle of reinvention and rejuvenation. Focusing forward, you reach a ground-breaking chapter of potential. You gain new information which helps provide you with a sense of clarity. You do feel able to develop a situation which holds promise. Exciting events are coming into your world. Directing your attention towards this area allows you to cross the threshold of a transition to a better place. You begin a voyage filled with wonder and excitement and joy. Several options are open for you to explore on this journey and you launch towards a delicate situation. Information arrives to inspire change. You are ready to embrace a new chapter of potential. This puts you towards an area which holds meaning to you. You are rewarded, quite unexpectedly with a situation which has you thinking about long-term plans.

DECEMBER WEEK FOUR

Life surprisingly supports your growth soon. This is ruled by fresh thinking, perception, and adventure. It is a beautiful time to launch towards a situation which holds promise. Intentions set soon turn into exciting opportunities. This brings you in contact with some eclectic individuals, and your social life moves forward. A bountiful chapter is ready to enter your life, your diligent efforts to focus on moving forward yields tangible results. A critical decision may this week allows you to pick up the pace and overcome limitations which have blocked progress. Expanded social activities lighten the mood and let you focus on spending time with your tribe. Networking and sharing ideas do place the focus on a particular area to develop soon. A burst of inspiration sets the stage for future progress for you. Your personal life takes center stage, and you embrace being able to plan for future improvement. The sun is lighting the path forward. This does suggest expansion occurring on a significant level. It allows you to draw incredible energy into your world and does take you to a happier chapter, which is highlighted by increasing abundance.

There is plenty to celebrate this season. You embrace spending time with your nearest and dearest and enjoy relaxing with your social set. It's a time of reflection about the year that has been, and the one that is yet to begin. Creating space to map out your goals does generate the air of a manifestation which arrives to support your vision.

Dear Stargazer,

I hope you have enjoyed planning your year with the stars utilizing Astrology and Zodiac influences. My zodiac star sign books are released each year which detail a monthly list of astrological events, and a weekly (four weeks to a month) horoscope. You can find me on my Facebook page where you can get personal astrology or intuitive readings.:

https://www.facebook.com/SiaSands

Feedback is welcomed and appreciated.

Many Blessings,

Sia Sands

www.ingramcontent.com/pod-product-compliance
Lightning Source LLC
Chambersburg PA
CBHW051216250726
48655CB00006B/2435